THE Haiku ECONOMIST

THE Haiku ECONOMIST

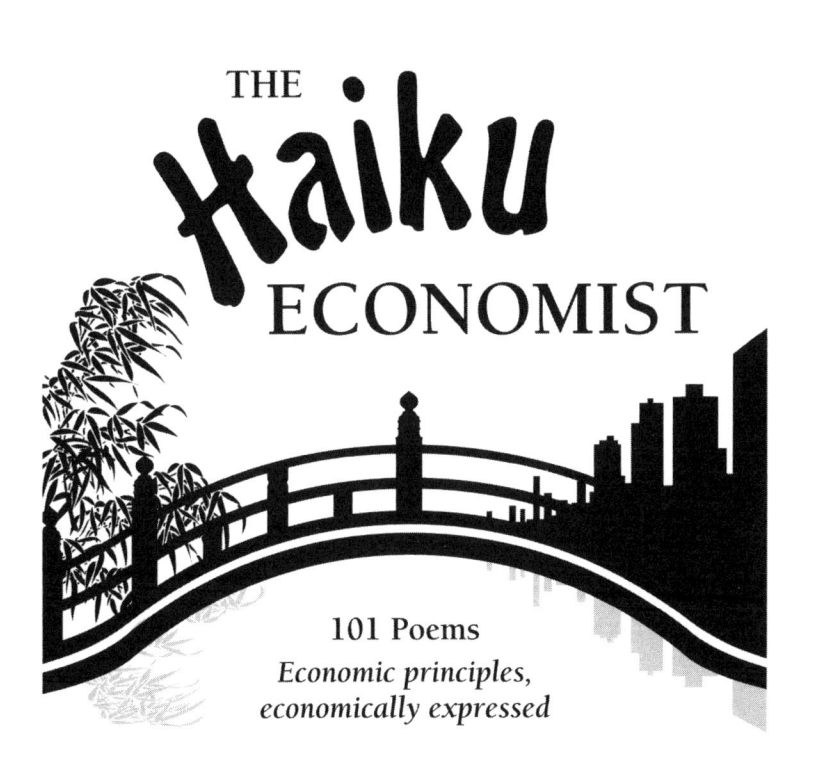

101 Poems

*Economic principles,
economically expressed*

JIM COX

THE ADVOCATES FOR SELF-GOVERNMENT
Cartersville, Georgia

Copyright © 2012 by Jim Cox

All rights reserved under International and Pan-American Copyright Conventions. No portion of this book may be reproduced, stored in a retrieval system, or transmitted in any form or by any means—electronic, mechanical, photocopy, recording, scanning, or other—except for brief quotations with attribution to the author, without prior written permission of the author or publisher.

Published in the United States of America
by the Advocates for Self-Government
269 Market Place Blvd. #106, Cartersville, Georgia 30121-2235
800-932-1776, info@TheAdvocates.org, www.TheAdvocates.org

FIRST EDITION
Published October 2012

Cox, Jim
The Haiku Economist: 101 Poems: Economic Principles, Economically Expressed

By Jim Cox

ISBN 978-0-9754326-7-9

1. Economics	2. Free-market economics	3. Austrian economics
4. Libertarianism	5. Haiku	6. Poetry
I. Title	II. Cox, Jim	

Cover design by Amy Landheer, JPL Design Solutions
Book design, typography, and editing by Elizabeth C. Brierly
Manufactured in the United States of America

To Cherie

Also by the Author

The Concise Guide to Economics

*Minimum Wage, Maximum Damage:
How the Minimum Wage Law Destroys Jobs,
Perpetuates Poverty, and Erodes Freedom*

Also from the Publisher

Libertarianism in One Lesson
by David Bergland

*Liberty A to Z:
872 Libertarian Soundbites You Can Use Right Now!*
by Harry Browne

Secrets of Libertarian Persuasion
by Michael Cloud

Unlocking More Secrets of Libertarian Persuasion
by Michael Cloud

Short Answers to the Tough Questions, Expanded Edition
by Dr. Mary J. Ruwart

*Discovering Self-Government:
A Bible-Based Study Guide*
by Virgil L. Swearingen

Contents

Prose

Acknowledgements 9
Publisher's Preface, Sharon Harris 11
Introduction, Art Carden 13
How It All Started, Randy Sharian 17

The Haiku

I. Definitions 19
II. People, Organizations, Economists 27
III. Principles 55
IV. Money 101
V. The Federal Reserve 119

A Skosh More

Who's Who in the History of Economic Theory 135
Recommended Reading 139
What Is The Advocates for Self-Government? 141
About the Author 144

Acknowledgements

Writing a book is seldom a one-person effort. I received a lot of help.

I would like to thank Randy Sharian for confirming that I had, in fact, produced a valid haiku the first time I tried to do so, and for listening to my concerns, over the months of preparation leading to the publication of this book.

Because it was Facebook where I originally posted my haiku, I'd like to thank that dynamic entrepreneur Mark Zuckerberg, for having created such an extraordinary social networking tool.

Then, there are the Friends from my Facebook page, who hopefully enjoyed (or maybe, at times, endured) my postings poetic over a period of several months. Sharon Harris is one of those Friends—the one enthusiastic enough to suggest turning the collection of poems into a book.

Katherine Hanson, while interning at Advocates for Self-Government, did a fine job of checking each haiku to make sure it had the proper 5-7-5 sequence and made sense.

Finally, I'd like to thank Elizabeth Brierly for her great attention to detail and her excellent editing. She made this work much better than it would have otherwise been.

For anyone I have overlooked, I ask forgiveness, and I promise to correct my error in future editions.

–Jim Cox, the Haiku Economist
Tucker, Georgia

Publisher's Preface

In Jim's first book, *The Concise Guide to Economics*, he discussed major economic issues in brief chapters of just a couple of pages. But who knew he could be even more concise? Now he's delivering essential economic insights in a mere...17 syllables!

I love the paradoxical nature of the concept. After all, economics is ordinarily presented in a left-brain way: scientific, objective, detailed, logical. On the other hand, poetry is quite right-brained: ambiguous, subjective, subtle, emotional.

So in this unique volume, we have left and right, yin and yang, East and West!

In keeping with that theme, we've laid out the book to appeal to different ways of thinking. On the right-hand pages, you'll find the haiku. On the left-hand pages, you'll find more traditional, left-brain explorations of their meaning.

Haiku have been called "ah-ha!" poems, and the ones in this book are definitely that.

They will make you think, make you question, make you smile.

I could say much more, but to keep it appropriately short...

Read this unique book—
explore, enjoy, learn, and share
insights with others!

–Sharon Harris, President
The Advocates for Self-Government
Cartersville, Georgia

Introduction

Economics is incredibly important, yet those of us who study it and teach it for a living are constantly amazed at—and frustrated by—the general public's stubborn unwillingness to listen to what we have to say.

Consider international trade, for example. The law of *comparative advantage*—which shows that trade makes people better off—is one of the bedrock propositions of all economics, and indeed, free trade is one of the propositions on which, generally, economists across the intellectual spectrum agree. Despite the fact that there is consensus among professional economists of all ideological stripes that protectionism impoverishes us, politicians promise a never-ending stream of ways to interfere with trade, in order to protect American workers from foreign competition. This is just one example among many, such as federal agricultural subsidies, or cities' subsidies for stadiums and arenas.

What gives?

The explanation comes partly from *citizens' incentives*. Economics is hard to learn, and one person's learning more economics isn't likely to change public policy. As the economist Bryan Caplan discussed in his 2007 book, *The Myth of the Rational Voter*, citizens' incentives are such that people remain "rationally irrational" about economics: the policies they support are "irrational," in that they work against people's goals—someone who supports protectionism likely does so because he thinks it will make the U.S. more prosperous, when, in fact, it won't. But it is "rationally" that people hold these beliefs, because they are costly to change, and because the different views held by just one more person are unlikely to change public policy. People want prosperity, but with weak incentives to change their incorrect beliefs, they vote for protectionism instead.

As a professional economist, it's easy for me to cast aspersions upon the unlettered masses; however, the suppliers of economic wisdom are culpable, too. We take what is, in my humble opinion, the most fascinating subject in the world, and make it not merely unnecessarily difficult, but also...*boring*.

My own students usually have less-than-stellar things to say about their high school economics classes and teachers. Apparently, things aren't much better at the college level. "I hated economics; it was so *boring*," is typical of what I hear from audience members at my public speaking engagements.

Economics is more than an academic exercise. We're not debating how many angels can dance on the head of a pin. We're talking about the real lives of flesh-and-blood human beings.

What is to be done?

Enter Jim Cox's *The Haiku Economist*. Here Professor Cox makes a valuable contribution to economic literacy, using an art form I myself have employed to what I would like to think is great effect—see my video haiku posted at *LearnLiberty.org* (a project of the Institute for Humane Studies)—and he has done us all a great service by illustrating important economic principles, using a literary form which *itself* exemplifies important economic principles.

Writing haiku is a study in allocating scarce resources among competing ends: with the 5-7-5 syllable pattern, one must be choosy about what goes where. In having taken on this challenge, Professor Cox is in good company: Roosevelt University Trustee and Professor of Economics Stephen Ziliak—who should review this book!—has penned a number of excellent economics haiku and has been featured for his work.

In short, Professor Cox has taken that which many people find boring—even *dismal*—and has brought it to life in an artistic and engaging way. Students and teachers of the "dismal science" will find much in this book that inspires, that teaches—perhaps even that infuriates. We'll have a better world for it.

–Art Carden,
Assistant Professor of Economics, Samford University
and *Forbes.com* Columnist
Birmingham, Alabama

How It All Started

Late in the summer of 2009, a group of Decatur High School alumni, who'd been graduated in the late sixties and early seventies, began getting together weekly at a watering hole and restaurant known to its frequenters as "U-Joint." Regulars at these mid-week forays to the Oakhurst neighborhood on the south side of Decatur, Georgia included a former high school football hero turned rock 'n' roll hippie, a direct descendant of noted Georgia author Joel Chandler Harris, an English teacher, a retired sheriff's deputy, a libertarian (just one), and a former high school cheerleader named Linda, who distinguished herself early on as the literary conscience of the bunch.

Linda had become fascinated recently with the Japanese masters of the poetic art of haiku, and had been writing and sharing with the group some of her own creations. This inspired something of a haiku movement within the gang, and for several weeks, we would compose impromptu haiku, bursting into syllabification, either spontaneously or on command. We counted syllables on our fingers; rearranged words to fit the 5-7-5 format; laughed at the ridiculous and praised the sublime—of which a few somehow emerged.

It was around this time that members of our expanding group discovered Facebook. For several weeks, an inundation of haiku found its way from old friend to new friend to friend in the making. Not surprisingly, the group had not yet witnessed (nor expected, I daresay) any contribution from Jim Cox, economic purist and calculated logician. But one day, somewhere in the midst of all this syllable-rich cacophony, Jim sent me a poem, asking whether it was a valid haiku. It was. Jim then asserted to me in his straightforward manner, "I'm going to write one hundred haiku, and post one per day on Facebook."

Day after day, on Facebook, five poems appeared per week (Jim insisted on taking weekends off) under the banner of "The Haiku Economist." Facebook friends of Jim were treated to something like a compressed history and running commentary of libertarian economic thought—and now they've landed in this book for all to ponder.

As you will see, these ruminations, ramblings, and sensible sayings run the gamut from Adam Smith and Keynes to Tea Party times. Communists, socialists, deficit spenders, liberals, yellow- and blue-dog Democrats—not a one of these will cause you any pain as they are tallied one by one in the column of economic failures.

So, sit back and relax with a cigar, malt beverage, or caffeine-free diet drink. Jim wouldn't want you to stress out over any of these economics nuggets, but rather, enjoy them freely as they are freely being given to you *de profundis*: the truth, the economist's bible, the rightful American way!

–Randy Sharian
Atlanta, Georgia

~ 1 ~

Definitions

Austrian business-cycle theory cites the price-distorting effects of an artificial increase in the money supply as the ill of the business cycle, and the resulting depression as the necessary correction to put resources back in line with consumer preferences.

Today's *fiat money* (in contrast to *commodity money*) is valuable only because it was valuable yesterday, back to the point when it was commodity money.

"Depression" is the
correcting of previous
times of inflation.

Regression theorem:
Fiat money has value
only from the past.

A house is properly understood as a consumer good, not an investment good; houses lose value, like all consumer items, from wear and tear, and obsolescence.

In the technical jargon of microeconomics, a firm has monopoly power if it faces a falling demand curve. The older, common-sense theory of monopoly is an exclusive grant of privilege from government.

House: Big, expensive
asset, slowly but surely
falling to pieces.

A "monopoly"
is not simply facing a
falling demand curve!

Jim Cox

The interests of producers and consumers are aligned, via profits.

Two methodologies compete as the basis of economics: deductive reasoning from self-evident truths, and empiricism—the gathering of facts.

Profit: The reward
for moving goods to higher,
more valued uses.

Empiricism
it ain't; deductive reason,
'tis, economics.

~ II ~

People, Organizations, Economists

Jim Cox

The best-known theory of a class conflict is that of Karl Marx, in the form of *owners of capital vs. laborers*, but libertarians constructed it years earlier, along the lines of *net tax payers and net tax consumers*.

Norman Borlaug provided for far more people than did the far more celebrated Mother Teresa, through his work in developing high-yield "super crops." He is credited with having saved 1 billion people from starvation.

The real class struggle:
tax payers and tax eaters.
Marx mistook it all.

More than Mother T.,
Borlaug's "green revolution"
ended suffering.

Both John Law, in the early 1700s, and John Maynard Keynes, in the 1930s, believed that artificial increases in the money supply could cure what ails an economy.

In the 1920s, Mises and Hayek argued that socialism is incapable of allocating resources efficiently. The socialists eventually conceded their points, but persisted in their ideology, nonetheless.

John Law, John Maynard:
Money cranks who knew only
one answer, each time.

Mises and Hayek
won calculation debate.
The socialists lost!

Before the Keynesian revolution of the 1930s, it was widely regarded as wrong to run deficits. Keynes excused deficits, and now we have them as accepted and routine.

A mixed economy is one with elements of socialism and capitalism, so you can be either a victim or a victimizer.

Deficits, once wrong,
Keynes said are perfectly fine.
What a legacy!

"Your choice," said Ayn Rand:
"Sucker or a bloodsucker?"
—in our mixed system.

Carl Menger of Austria founded
the Austrian school of thought
in the 1870s; he was an
Aristotelian in his approach.

Successful unions are composed
of skilled (highly paid) workers;
they raise their pay rates only
by lowering the pay rates of
the non-unionized (unskilled).

Menger founded the
Austrians with a grounding
in Aristotle.

Said Milton Friedman:
Unions don't cause high pay; high
pay causes unions.

> In direct opposition are the views of Mises and Keynes: Keynes dismissed concerns about the long-run effects of his theories with the phrase, "In the long run we're all dead."

> The "put" was the correctly assumed view that Alan Greenspan, as Federal Reserve chairman, would engineer low interest rates to assure profitability in the stock market.

Mises: "Free markets!"
"No," Keynes said. "Government? Yes."
Keynes' long-run is here.

There was no need to
worry about investments
with the Greenspan Put.

Jim Cox

> The National Inflation Association, through their website, is preparing Americans with facts, figures, and history, so they can protect themselves from the threat of hyperinflation.

> John Maynard Keynes advocated zero interest rates to euthanize the rentier and to keep an economy artificially going at full tilt, overlooking the vital role actual prices play in the rational allocation of scarce resources..

The Haiku Economist

The N.I.A. is
preparing Americans
for high inflation.

Keynes wanted to have
a zero interest rate—
no grasp of prices?

Milton Friedman had simple, straightforward statements about a number of things. In this case, he identified the source of price inflation as an increase in the money supply.

Among other issues on which they disagreed, Thomas Jefferson believed in frugality and balanced budgets, while Alexander Hamilton thought federal debt was a way to bind the country together.

Friedman: Inflation
everywhere, and always a
monetary thing.

Jefferson stood for
balanced budgets, versus
Hamilton for debt.

To explain the errant ways of too many economists, Murray Rothbard created the maxim that economists specialize in the subject at which they are worst.

The Ludwig von Mises Institute is the leading proponent of Austrian economics, via its website.

Rothbard's Law: It's known,
economists specialize
in their worst topic!

The L. V. M. I.,
bringing Austrian theory
to people worldwide.

Cato Institute is headquartered in Washington, D.C., a location often referred to as the "belly of the beast" (the federal government).

The Phillips Curve postulated a trade-off between inflation and unemployment which is false, despite having been standard economic theory for several decades.

Cato Institute
working in the belly of
the D of C beast.

Phillips Curve: What a
crock! Generations misled.
No trade-off at all!

Jim Cox

> Joseph Schumpeter coined the term "creative destruction" to describe the market phenomenon of newer, better products and services making previous ones obsolete.

> During the 1970s, high inflation was accompanied by high unemployment—an impossibility, according to Keynes. Despite this failure, Keynesian theory has made a major comeback.

Markets will progress
by creative destruction,
as Schumpeter said.

Seventies should have
put an end to Age of Keynes.
Instead, he's baaack!

Jim Cox

> Artificial run-ups in the economy set the economy on a path ending in a bust, as depicted in EconStories' music video, "Fear the Boom and Bust: A Hip-Hop Macro Anthem."

> Ludwig von Mises stated that government will intervene further in an economy to correct the unintended effects of the previous intervention.

The boom plants the seeds
for the later bust—see the
Boom-Bust video!

It's known as Mises'
Law: Intervention begets
next intervention.

A good economist takes into consideration not only the visible effects of a policy, but the unseen and unintended consequences of that policy.

Keynesians don't recognize malinvestments—they never use the term. In their aggregate-based system, totals are what matters, not individual use of resources for specific purposes.

Bastiat: famous
for the distinction of the
seen and the unseen.

Is "malinvestment"
a term unknown to mainstream
Keynesian theorists?

The most fundamental of Marxian economic theories is the "labor theory of value," which is fallacious; so all that follows is fallacious as well.

With the Keynesian multiplier, one generates additional income purely by spending. No need to work; just spend and enjoy!

On labor theory
of value, Marx ran aground
economic thought.

Keynes' multiplier:
Beats working for a living.
It's stones into bread!

~ III ~

Principles

Greater demand for electricity during summer months causes prices to rise. If prices were not allowed to rise, the quantity demanded would exceed the quantity supplied, resulting in an electricity shortage.

One of the functions of advertising is to serve as a reminder to otherwise busy consumers, who may have forgotten about products they liked in the past.

Summer rates go up.
Supply and demand, you know,
or else, shortages.

My old favorite
candy, spotted on the shelf.
Thanks, advertising!

Artificial increases in the money supply bid up the values of items such as stocks and houses; such bubbles always burst.

The comedian denounced communism for its lack of consumer choice among suppliers.

Stock market, high-tech
stocks, housing, clunkers, bubbles—
all from phony funds.

Lenny Bruce said it:
Communism, just like one big
phone company, man.

Public housing is the least appealing housing; there's no reason to expect that public (*i.e.*, government) health care would be of any higher quality.

By pricing the labor of low-skilled workers too high, the minimum wage destroys job opportunities for those very workers.

Government health care:
not any more attractive
than public housing.

Minimum wage wrecks
job opportunities for
low-skilled poor people.

> Free prices coordinate the activities of buyers and sellers, resulting in a well-ordered economy; central planning results in chaos.

> By triggering a rise in prices of goods threatened with a reduction in supply, speculators alert everyone, early, to that future reduction.

Free prices result
in an organic order,
but top-down doesn't.

Speculators do
what smoke detectors do, too:
warn us of bad things.

In their first two years in Plymouth, the Pilgrims used an "all for one and one for all" production and consumption system. More than half died.

After two years, the Pilgrims switched to an individual-responsibility system, and their community thrived.

At first, Pilgrims tried
a socialized production.
They nearly all starved.

The Pilgrims changed to
private-property basis,
and flourish they did!

Trade is based on valuing what is given up less than what is received. Accounting records must balance, so they do not acknowledge the surpluses from trades.

"Cash for clunkers" paid for the destruction of older, cheaper cars, making the prices of used cars increase, burdening low-income car shoppers.

Trade deficits are
accounting statistics that
don't account for gains.

The "cash for clunkers"
program destroyed the used cars.
That's good for the poor?

Textbooks typically point out that the federal government is different from individuals, in not having to fear going bankrupt, since the feds have the power to create money—even to the point of making the dollar worthless.

Textbooks typically point out that the federal government is different from individuals, in not having to fear going bankrupt, since the feds have the power to tax—even to the point of bankrupting the taxpayers.

Don't you worry; your
government won't go bankrupt.
They'll kill the dollar.

Don't you worry; your
government won't go bankrupt.
They'll tax you broke, first.

With the national debt sailing past $16 trillion at the time of this writing (a record-breaking number), each American citizen's share is over $51,000.

You can keep tabs on the debt clock at www.USDebtClock.org.

In the 1920s, socialist theoreticians in Russia attempted to outlaw prices in order to centrally plan their economy; instead, they produced economic chaos.

The Haiku Economist

The National Debt
sixteen trillion—your share just
as staggering, too.

The Socialists called
for removal of prices,
money; got chaos.

Long Term Capital Management, a Connecticut-based hedge fund, failed in 1998, and was bailed out through a plan engineered by the Federal Reserve.

Firms are allowed to fail, except for those with political connections so strong that they are deemed essential.

L.T.C.M. failed:
Started the bailouts we still
suffer from today.

"Too big to fail" means
actually, in fact, too
connected to fail.

Among the teachings of economics is that actions have consequences that are not a part of the intentions of the actors.

Firms maximize their profits by producing the quantity of output at which marginal costs (the cost of producing one more unit) and marginal revenues (the revenue generated by selling one more unit) match.

The Haiku Economist

Great econ lesson:
The law of unintended
type consequences.

At marginal costs
and marginal revenue,
profits maximize.

When unions press firms for wages higher than the market would have determined, fewer union workers will be hired at that higher wage, and non-unionized workers will suffer from the increased supply in their industries, resulting in lower wages: worker vs. worker.

"Scabs" are workers who seek a much-needed job at the firm where other workers are on strike. That the first group is called "scab" shows that workers do not all have common interests.

Unions get more pay;
others, less. It's a worker-
versus-worker thing.

Job strikers call job
seekers "scabs." Some working-class
solidarity!

Opportunity cost—that which one can no longer do with a resource, because that resource has been used for another purpose—is the actual price paid for everything.

Charity shifts around existing wealth; production creates additional wealth.

Great econ lesson:
Opportunity cost: the
 actual price paid.

Production does more
to alleviate world needs
 than does charity.

Economists have pointed out
that bombs and rent controls
have the same effect:
destroyed buildings.

Opportunity costs are the
ultimate price paid for things,
because the money and time
are no longer available
to be spent on other things.

A destroyed city:
Is it from bomb damage, or
is it rent controls?

Opportunity
costs mean more of A, less of
B, as in "trade-off."

> Rather than protecting the public, licensing is a means to make sure the incomes of licensed individuals are protected from competition.

> Those with an income close to the poverty level will be taxed into poverty when sales, gasoline, and other taxes are added to the cost of goods.

The Haiku Economist

What is licensing?
Protecting the licensed from
those low selling prices!

Sales tax, and others,
literally do tax some
into poverty.

Haiti is a have-not country, because it doesn't have economic freedom.

Source:
Heritage Foundation's 2012 Index of Economic Freedom;
Heritage.org/index/ranking

Wall Street firms are closely tied to Washington, D.C. powers, and are handsomely rewarded for those ties.

Index of Econ
Freedom reveals Haiti is
very nearly last!

Oh, what a cozy
relationship it is, for
D.C. and Wall Street.

> Profits are a reward for producing what consumers want, so businesses are rewarded in proportion to the degree they please consumers.

> State regulation restricts competition and thus sacrifices consumers, who benefit when markets are brimming with competitors. Big businesses hire lawyers and accountants to help them comply, but their smaller competitors usually can't afford it.

Pursuit of profits
brings interests of buyers,
sellers together.

Gov regulation
teams the state and businesses
against consumers.

"Perfect competition" theory
is theory run amok,
so far from reality
as to be irrelevant.

Congress has full authority
to choose which spending to
undertake; none is off limits
for reconsideration.

Thinking in terms of
perfect competition is
not reality.

All Congressional
spending is at-discretion
spending...all of it.

"Stimulus spending" is nothing but transfer payments by another name.

All government spending is at the expense of the rest of the economy, whether funded by taxes or not.

Stimulus: Money
from Paul, to give to someone
with the name Peter.

The burden of Gov
is total spending, not just
total taxation.

Recovery is a process of reallocating resources in line with consumer preferences; for the market to accomplish that, failed businesses must be allowed to fail.

The all-important concept of the rivalry between firms, which is attracting consumers, is nowhere to be found in graphs depicting perfect competition.

For recovery,
let failed businesses fail, and
then consumers rule.

Competition is
rivalry in attracting
consumers, not graphs.

By depriving people of the choice they would have found to be their best option, people's alleged benefactors are harming them.

Starting from scarcity, economics develops, and sometimes arrives at, counter-intuitive conclusions.

No-good do-gooders
do more harm than good, with their
interferences.

Economics: The
study of scarce resources,
shocking conclusions.

When investments are made in products or services that prove to be unpopular, resources have been wasted. Better to cut losses and move investments to areas supported by consumers.

When people act, they unintentionally create outcomes that appear to have been designed.

Malinvestments need
to be liquidated, so
good ones can resume.

Market is result
of human action, but not
of human design.

Tax collections have increased tremendously over the years—for example, from $1.03 trillion in 1990 to $2.7 trillion in 2008— much more than enough to have closed the deficits.

If raising taxes
cured deficits, it would have
happened long ago.

~ IV ~

Money

When people are allowed to freely choose what to use as a medium of exchange, gold is overwhelmingly their choice. But the U.S. government has thwarted such a choice, by forcing fiat money (backed by nothing).

Prices convey meaningful information. The artificial increase in the money supply, which is inflation, sends out faulty signals, which result in malinvestments in capital.

Gold is people's choice
in money, not this fiat.
Here we are, despite.

Inflation does more
than raise prices; distorts all
capital, as well.

Franklin Delano Roosevelt took the U.S. off the gold standard, domestically, in 1933; Nixon took the U.S. off the gold standard, internationally, in 1971. The dollar's value fell precipitously, after and since both events.

Since gold must be extracted from mines, not created with printing presses as is government-decreed money, it holds its value, while dollars are inflated to near worthlessness.

The Haiku Economist

Once mighty dollar
laid low by FDR and
Nixon, tyrants both.

Gold maintains value.
This fiat is fraudulent;
gold is true money.

Jim Cox

> Inflation is not neutral;
> it has redistributive effects,
> taking from some and
> benefiting others.

> In 1965, U.S. coins were
> debased, as copper and
> zinc began being substituted
> for their silver content.

Inflation takes from
last who receive it; gives to
those first to get it.

Silver coins once, now
sandwich tokens, since sixties'
debasing money.

The banking system operates on fractional reserves of depositors' deposits, creating claims by two people for the same dollars. Customers panic, at times, trying to claim their rightful money, resulting in bank runs.

As Menger proved, money did not originate by vote, government fiat, or anything else but trade of useful goods.

Fractional reserves:
two claims on same deposit.
So bank runs, of course.

Money from useful
goods did not originate
in another way.

The U.S. went off the gold standard domestically in 1933, and internationally in 1971. The only thing backing the dollar is more unredeemable dollars.

Paper money can be and has been created to the point of hyperinflation, and, unlike gold, has no inherent value.

What backs the dollar?
Not gold, not silver—nothing
but more of the same.

Unlike the dollar,
governments cannot print gold.
That's gold's great virtue.

When money was gold and
silver, anyone could save
by holding such a coin,
in full confidence that
it would have value later.
Now, with fiat money losing
its value steadily, everyone
has to guess what to invest in.

There is no objective definition
for how much of something
it takes to constitute "hoarding";
it's just a preference.

The Haiku Economist

Old days, save a gold
or silver coin. No more. Now
guess where to invest.

"Hoarding" money is
just holding more than others
think you should, you know?

Inflation is not an increase in prices, but an increase in the money supply—which, in turn, causes prices to rise.

Bad investments (those not based on consumer demand) come from bad interest rates (those not based on consumer demand).

Inflation: Increase
in money supply. Increased
prices? Just the effect.

Malinvestments come
from artificial excess
in money supply.

Jim Cox

> Since fiat money (in contrast to commodity money) can be created without limit, it naturally follows that hyperinflation is the end result.

Hyperinflation:
A predictable result
of fiat money.

~ V ~

The Federal Reserve

Jim Cox

Inflation is an increase in the money supply, as engineered by the Federal Reserve Bank system. The increased money supply forces prices upward. Congressman Ron Paul wrote the best-selling book *End the Fed*.

By inflating the money supply—and thereby devaluing the existing dollars—the limited funds of orphans and widows are undermined.

Inflating money.
Prices rise; who is to blame?
"End the Fed," says Paul.

The Fed's history:
Robbing widows and orphans
since 1914.

Jim Cox

> Artificially low interest rates encourage home buying and construction, resulting in a boom in prices, and ultimately a boom—as in *explosion*—of values.

> Since the founding of the Federal Reserve System in 1913, the value of the dollar has fallen by 95 percent.

Artificially
low interest rates always make
house prices go boom.

The dollar was one,
but now worth 5 little cents—
all thanks to the Fed.

Ben Bernanke, Chairman of the Federal Reserve Bank, made clear his commitment to inflate the money supply, by saying that he would, if necessary, drop the newly created dollars by helicopter.

Like illegal counterfeiters, the Federal Reserve creates currency, but instead of a "crime," it is called "monetary policy."

"Helicopter Ben"
we call him, because he will
inflate without end.

Fed counterfeiting:
"monetary policy,"
they like to call it.

Jim Cox

> The Federal Reserve Bank, created in 1913, was followed sixteen years later by the Great Depression. Now, after another several decades, has the Fed engineered an even worse downturn?

> It is an absolute truth that the Federal Reserve creates inflation, though it claims to lead the fight against it.

The Fed, following
the Great Depression with the
Greater Depression?

The Fed is the source,
not the cure, for inflation.
Take that to the bank!

Jim Cox

As Federal Reserve chairman, Ben Bernanke oversaw the creation of $2 trillion, in what is now called QE1 (Quantitative Easing 1), robbing value from everyone's pre-existing dollars.

The Federal Reserve determines the money supply, which is half of all transactions, so we should be privy to what they have, and what they are doing.

One trillion dollars
created makes Bernanke
biggest thief around!

The most powerful
econ force in U.S., Fed,
should be audited!

Jim Cox

In response to the economic downturn, Federal Reserve chairman Ben Bernanke increased reserves by $2 trillion, promising an exit strategy to remove all of that money, but has since undertaken an injection of another $600 billion.

The Haiku Economist

Has Ben Bernanke
swallowed a fly with his
Q. E. 1 and 2?

A Skosh More

Who's Who in the History of Economic Theory

Adam Smith (1723 1790): Scottish author of *The Wealth of Nations* 1776; developed free trade theory and an appreciation for the division of labor; set back marginal utility analysis with cost of production theory of value; Classical.

Anne-Robert-Jacques Turgot (1727-1781): French author of *Reflections* 1766; established marginal utility analysis; Physiocrat.

Jean Baptiste Say (1767-1832): French author of *Treatise on Political Economy* 1803; originator of "Say's Law"; Classical.

David Ricardo (1772-1823): English author of *Principles of Political Economy* 1817; originator of the law of comparative advantage; his rent theory influenced George; his wage theory influenced Marx; Classical.

Karl Marx (1818-1883): German transplant to England; newspaper writer and author of *The Communist Manifesto* 1848 and *Das Kapital* 1867, arguing for collective ownership, determinist theory of history, and the labor theory of value; Communist.

Henry George (1839-1897): American author of *Progress and Poverty* 1879, based on Ricardo's theory of rent; an advocate of a single tax on land; advocate of free trade.; Georgist.

Carl Menger (1840-1921): Austrian author of *The Principles of Economics* 1871, re-establishing marginal utility analysis (the marginal revolution); considered the founder of the Austrian school of economics.

John Bates Clark (1847-1938): American author of *Distribution of Wealth* 1899, establishing the marginal productivity theory of income distribution; Neo-classical/Institutionalist.

Eugen Bohm-Bawerk (1851-1914): Austrian author of *Capital and Interest* 1884 and *Karl Marx and the Close of His System* 1896, emphasizing "roundabout production" and disputing the labor theory of value; Austrian.

Thorstein Veblen (1858-1920): American author of *The Theory of the Leisure Class* 1899; coined the term "conspicuous consumption" and ridiculed the law of diminishing marginal utility; Institutionalist.

Ludwig von Mises (1881-1973): Austrian transplant to U.S.; author of *The Theory of Money and Credit* 1912 and *Human Action* 1949; applied marginal utility analysis to money, developing a new theory of business cycles; with Hayek, disputed the possibility of socialist planning; Austrian.

Joseph Schumpeter (1883-1950): Austrian transplant to U.S.; author of *Capitalism, Socialism and Democracy* 1942 and *History of Economic Analysis* 1954; originated term "creative destruction" to describe capitalism; "methodologically tolerant" Austrian.

John Maynard Keynes (1885-1946): English Lord; author of *The General Theory* 1936, establishing a "macroeconomics" and an underconsumptionist theory of the business cycle; the most influential economist of the twentieth century; Keynesian.

Friedrich A. Hayek (1899-1992): Austrian transplant to U.S.; devotee of Mises; author of *The Road to Serfdom* 1944 and *The Fatal Conceit* 1989; with Mises, disputed the possibility of socialist planning; Nobel Prize 1974; Austrian.

John Kenneth Galbraith (1908-2006): American author of *The Affluent Society* 1957 and *The New Industrial State* 1973; disputed the value of advertising and of competition among oligopolists; follower of Veblen; Institutionalist.

Milton Friedman (1912-2006): American author of *Capitalism and Freedom* 1962 and *Free to Choose* 1980; emphasized the connection between economic and political freedom, and the importance of the money supply in the macroeconomy; Nobel Prize 1976; Monetarist.

Paul Samuelson (1915-2009): American Keynesian: "Keynes' Paul," author of the best-selling and first Keynesian text, *Economics* 1949; Nobel Prize 1970; Keynesian.

James Buchanan (1919-): American author of *The Calculus of Consent* 1962; founder of Public Choice economic theory applying self-interest motivations to all, including government officials; Nobel Prize 1986; Public Choicer.

Robert Lucas (1937-): American influenced by Milton Friedman at University of Chicago; originator of rational expectations theory; Nobel Prize 1994; Monetarist/Rational Expectations.

Recommended Reading

For the reader whose interest has been piqued, here is a succinct collection that will help expand your understanding of the poems' principles.

~

***The Concise Guide to Economics*, by Jim Cox.** (Auburn, Alabama: Ludwig von Mises Institute, 2007.)

***Minimum Wage, Maximum Damage*, by Jim Cox.** (Cartersville, Georgia: The Advocates for Self-Government, 2004.)

~

***Bright Promises, Dismal Performance*, by Milton Friedman**. (New York: Harcourt Press, 1983.)

***Capitalism: The Unknown Ideal*, by Ayn Rand.** (New York, New York: New American Library, 1967.)

***Defending the Undefendable*, by Walter Block.** (New York: Fleet Press, 1976.)

***Economics in One Lesson,* by Henry Hazlitt.** (New Rochelle, New York: Arlington House, 1979.)

***The Essential Ludwig von Mises,* by Murray Rothbard.** (Auburn, Alabama: Ludwig von Mises Institute, 1983.)

***The Incredible Bread Machine,* by Susan Love Brown, Karl Keating, David Mellinger, Patrea Post, Stuart Smith, and Catriona Tudor.** (San Diego, California: World Research Inc., 1974.)

***The Making of Modern Economics: The Lives and Ideas of the Great Thinkers,* by Mark Skousen.** Armonk, New York: M. E. Sharpe, 2001.)

***What Everyone Should Know About Economics and Prosperity,* by James D. Gwartney and Richard L. Stroup**. (Tallahassee, Florida: The Fraser Institute, 1993.)

***What Has Government Done to Our Money?,* by Murray Rothbard.** (Auburn, Alabama: Ludwig von Mises Institute, 1990.)

***Whatever Happened to Penny Candy?* by Richard Maybury**. (Placerville, California: Bluestocking Press, 1989.)

What Is The Advocates for Self-Government?

The Advocates has made invaluable contributions to the freedom cause.... I continue to be impressed by [their] work.
—Congressman Ron Paul

Since 1985, the Advocates has worked to create a free society by empowering lovers of liberty to become highly effective and successful at taking the ideas of liberty to the world.

Libertarians in many different organizations benefit from our expertise in activism, communications, and psychology by using our products, programs, and services:

- **Tools** like the World's Smallest Political Quiz, which replaces the outmoded "left-right" line with a new and more inclusive political map, and makes it easy for individuals to find who agrees with them most in the world of politics...
- **Books** like *Short Answers to the Tough Questions* and *Libertarianism in One Lesson*...
- **Newsletters** like the *Liberator Online,* our popular, free email newsletter...
- **Speakers** like Sharon Harris, Michael Cloud, and Mary Ruwart, who conduct communication trainings, and...
- **Websites** like *LibertarianAnswers.com*, *Libertarianism.com*, and now Professor Cox's *HaikuEconomist.com*—where you'll find more haiku, enticing discussion, and contests!

Learn more! Visit *TheAdvocates.org* or call us at 800-932-1776.

~ Haiku and Notes ~

~ Haiku and Notes ~

About the Author

Jim Cox, the Haiku Economist, is the author of two previous books: *The Concise Guide to Economics* and *Minimum Wage, Maximum Damage*.

His articles and commentaries have appeared in numerous publications, including *Great Ideas for Teaching Economics*, the *Atlanta Journal and Constitution*, the *San Diego Business Journal*, and the *Orange County Register*.

He is a member of the Board of Scholars for the Virginia Institute for Public Policy and an adjunct scholar of the Ludwig von Mises Institute. He is a past president of the Georgia Association of Economics and Finance, and has served as a Fellow of the Institute for Humane Studies, as an officer in the Georgia Political Science Association, and on the Academic Board of Advisors for the Georgia Public Policy Foundation.

He is an associate professor of economics and political science and has taught the principles of economics since 1979.

When not teaching, writing, or composing haiku on economics, Jim enjoys reading, table tennis, golf, weekly team trivia with friends, and traveling with his wife, Cherie.

You can contact Jim and enjoy further discussion of economics and haiku at *www.HaikuEconomist.com*.